TAKE-OFF!

Bug Books

FLY

**Karen Hartley, Chris Macro
and Philip Taylor**

Heinemann
LIBRARY

www.heinemann.co.uk

Visit our website to find out more information about Heinemann Library books.

To order:

☎ Phone 44 (0) 1865 888066

📠 Send a fax to 44 (0) 1865 314091

💻 Visit the Heinemann Bookshop at www.heinemann.co.uk to browse our catalogue and order online.

First published in Great Britain by Heinemann Library,
Halley Court, Jordan Hill, Oxford OX2 8EJ,
a division of Reed Educational and Professional Publishing Ltd.
Heinemann is a registered trademark of Reed Educational and Professional Publishing Ltd.

OXFORD MELBOURNE AUCKLAND
JOHANNESBURG BLANTYRE GABORONE
IBADAN PORTSMOUTH (NH) USA CHICAGO

© Reed Educational and Professional Publishing Ltd 2001

Designed by Ron Kamen
Illustrated by Alan Fraser at Pennant Illustration
Originated by Ambassador Litho ltd
Printed by South China Printing in Hong Kong/China

ISBN 0 431 01821 9 (hardback)　　ISBN 0 431 01826 X (paperback)
05 04 03 02 01　　　　　　　　　05 04 03 02 01
10 9 8 7 6 5 4 3 2 1　　　　　　　10 9 8 7 6 5 4 3 2 1

British Library Cataloguing in Publication Data

Hartley, Karen
　　Fly. – (Bug books) (Take-off!)
　　1.Flies – Juvenile literature
　　I.Title II.Macro, Chris, 1940– III.Taylor. Philip, 1949–
　　595.7'7

Acknowledgements

The publishers would like to thank the following for permission to reproduce photographs:
Ardea London: Alan Weaving p.9, JL Mason p.7, P Morris p.10, p.11, p.21, Pascal Goetgheluck p.24, p.28; Bruce Coleman: Felix Labhardt p.18, Jane Burton p.16; FLPA: B Borell p.4, p.25; Heather Angel p.15; Nature Photographers Ltd: Nicholas Phelps Brown p.23; NHPA: P Sorensen & J Olsen p.17, Stephen Dalton p.12, p.13, p.20, p.26; Oxford Scientific Films: Andrew Plumptre p.22, Avril Ramage p.5, p.14, Bob Fredrick p.19, GI Bernard p.8, KG Vock p.6, London Scientific Films p.29, Stephen Dalton p.27.

Cover photograph reproduced with permission of Bruce Coleman.

Our thanks to Sue Graves and Hilda Reed for their advice and expertise in the preparation of this book.

Every effort has been made to contact copyright holders of any material reproduced in this book. Any omissions will be rectified in subsequent printings if notice is given to the publishers.

Contents

Any words appearing in the text in bold, **like this**, are explained in the Glossary.

What are flies?

A housefly.

Flies are **insects**. There are thousands of different kinds of flies. The flies that we see most are houseflies and bluebottles.

There are over 90,000 kinds of flies!

A maggot.

Maggots are often used as fish bait.

Young bluebottles and houseflies are called maggots. The maggots crawl around looking for food. They look like small, wriggling worms.

What do flies look like?

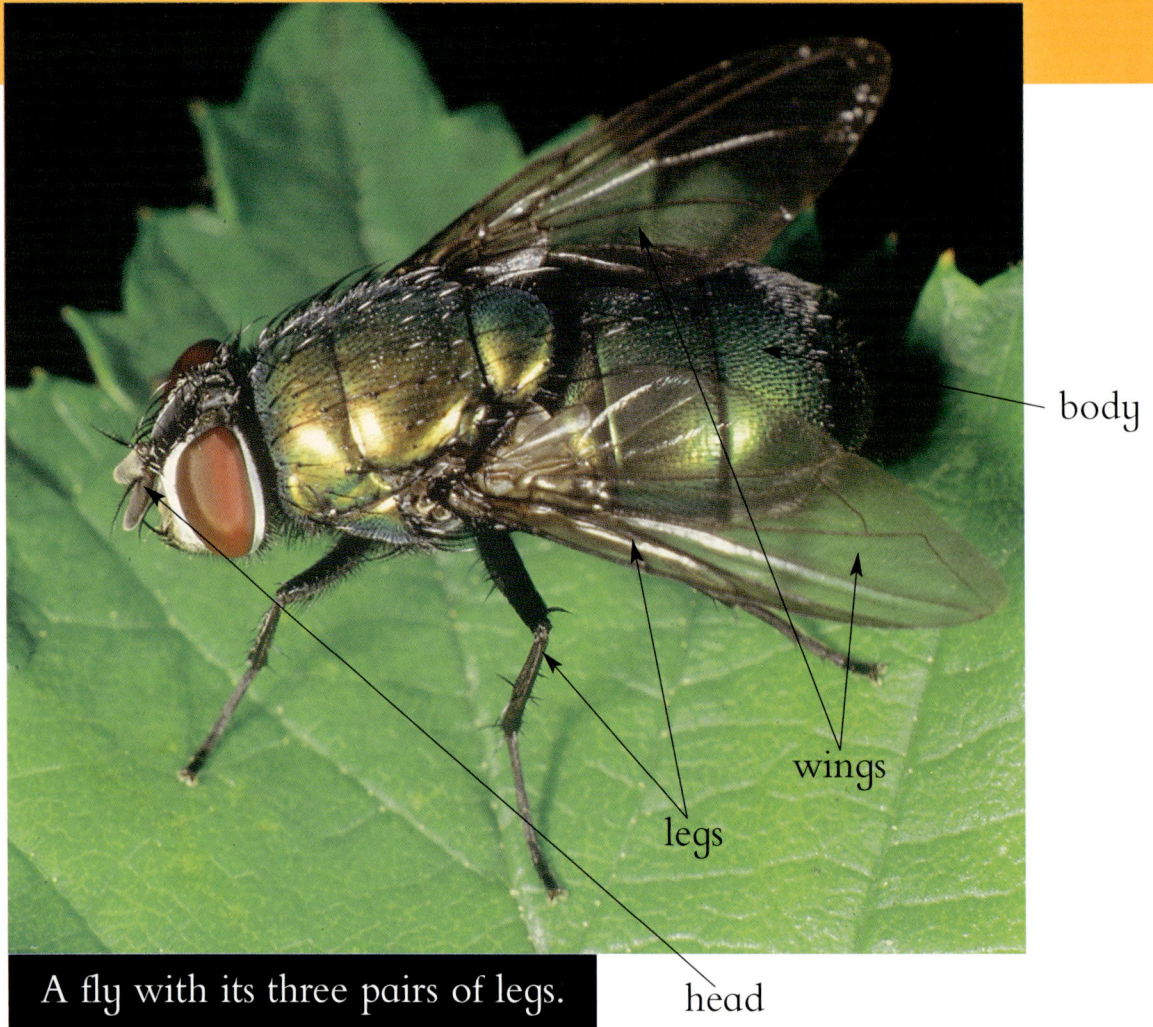

body

wings

legs

head

A fly with its three pairs of legs.

Flies have six legs. They have no mouth or teeth. They eat through a long tube at the front of the head. Flies have little holes in their bodies for breathing.

yellow markings

wings

feeler

legs

A hover fly.

A hover fly looks like a
wasp but it does not sting.

Flies have two **feelers** that they use for
smelling. The bluebottle and the greenbottle
are shiny. This hover fly has bright yellow
markings.

How big are flies?

A midge, which is a very small fly.

Some flies are very small. The midge that you can see here is not much bigger than a dot on a piece of paper.

Houseflies and bluebottles are fat and hairy. Crane flies are long and thin. This fly is called a robber fly. Some robber flies are as long as a man's finger!

A robber fly.

How are flies born?

A bluebottle laying eggs.

bluebottle

eggs

Houseflies and bluebottles lay their eggs in rotting, smelly vegetables or in bad meat. Sometimes flies lay their eggs in our food.

Maggots that have hatched from a fly's eggs.

The fly lays hundreds of eggs. After two days the eggs hatch into **larvae**.

A housefly can lay about 900 eggs at one time!

How do flies grow?

Fly pupae.

When the maggots get too big for their skins, they grow new ones and lose the old ones. This is called **moulting**. After about ten days the maggot changes into a **pupa**.

hard pupa case

An adult fly bursting out of the pupa case.

adult fly

Inside the pupa, the maggot changes into a fly. The pupa does not move. After about six days, the **adult** housefly bursts out of the hard pupa case.

What do flies eat?

Female flies on uncovered food.

female flies

Female houseflies and bluebottles sometimes come into our kitchens and nibble our food. **Male** bluebottles and houseflies suck up **nectar** from flowers.

Flies carry disease-spreading **germs**. Always remember to protect food from flies.

14

Flies spit juice onto their food. This makes the food very soft. The fly then sucks the food through its feeding tube. Some tiny flies suck blood from animals.

A fly on some food.

Which animals attack flies?

web

A spider that has trapped a fly in its web.

fly   spider

Spiders like to eat flies. The spiders catch the flies in their sticky webs. Birds and frogs also eat flies.

Spiders do not get stuck in their webs because they have oil on their feet.

fly

bird

A bird eating an adult fly.

Many animals eat the **larvae** of flies. Fish eat larvae that live near rivers and lakes. All sorts of birds like to eat maggots and adult flies. Maggots are the larvae of houseflies and bluebottles.

Where do flies live?

flies

animal droppings

Flies on animal droppings.

Flies live in most parts of the world. Some flies live in damp, shady places near water. Some like to live near plants, fruit and flowers. Some flies like to live on animal **droppings**.

An adult fly.

Many **adult** flies like to live near rotting food and rubbish. The **larvae** of different sorts of flies live in different places.

Some crane fly larvae live in **decaying** wood. Some live in mud or shallow pond water.

How do flies move?

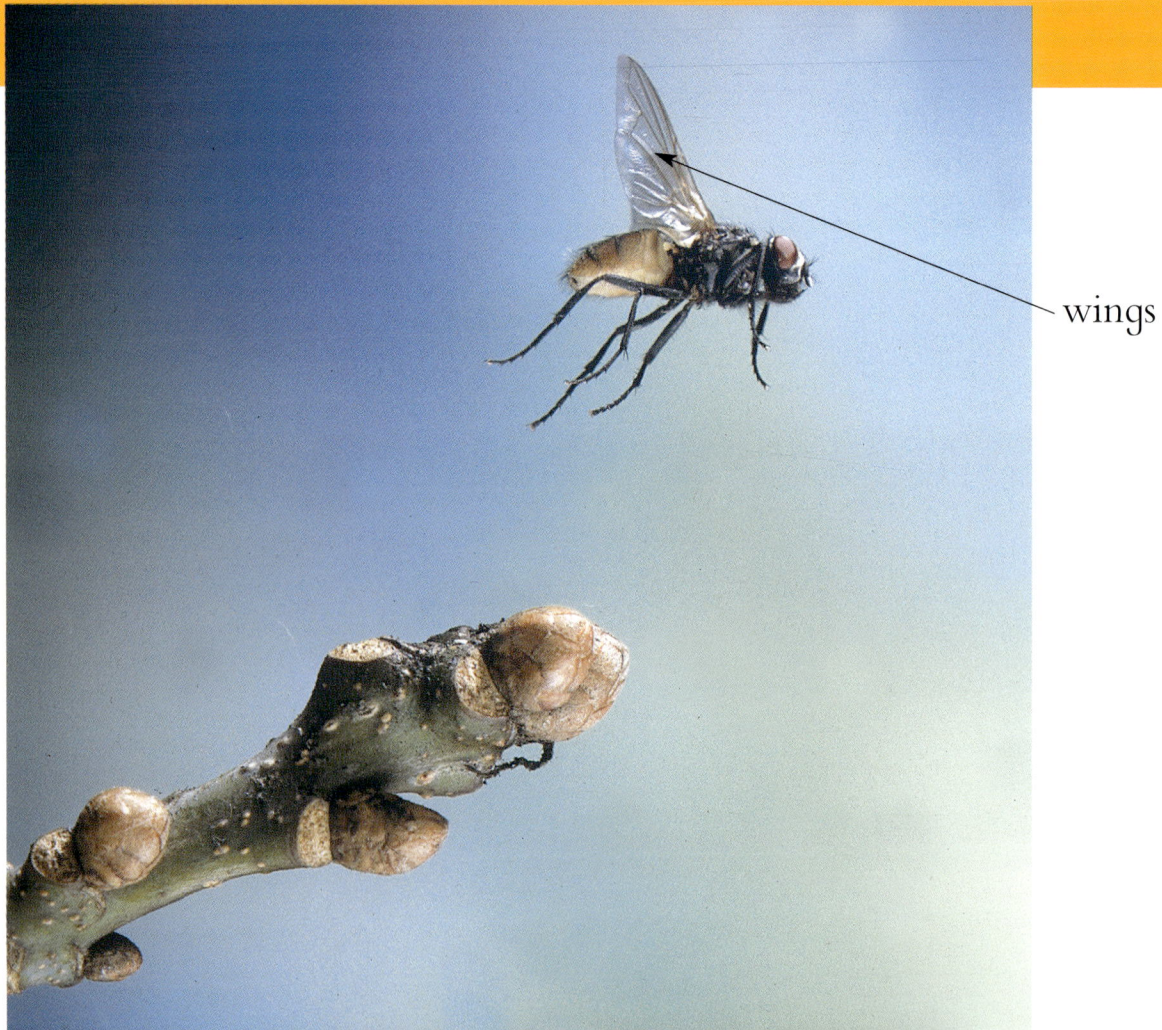

wings

A fly flapping its wings. This makes a buzzing sound.

Flies move very quickly through the air. The fly makes a buzzing sound. This is the noise of its wings flapping.

midges

A swarm of tiny midges.

Some very small flies move close together when they fly. This is called **swarming**.

How long do flies live?

pupa
case

adult housefly

This housefly will live for about 21 days.

The housefly will live for 21 days after it comes out of the **pupa**. Most flies die when the weather gets cold, but some flies go to sleep during the winter.

An adult midge.

The **adult** midge only lives for a day. This is just long enough for the **female** to **mate** and lay her eggs.

What do flies do?

flower

A male bluebottle sucking nectar from a flower.

male fly

Houseflies and bluebottles like to rest in the sun but they spend most of their time looking for food. It is only the **females** that come into our houses.

24

A fly on a dishcloth inside a house.

Many flies are **pests**. They pick up **germs** from dirty places. The flies bring the dirt and germs into our houses and on to our food.

Some flies carry very dangerous diseases. In Africa, the tsetse fly carries sleeping sickness.

How are flies special?

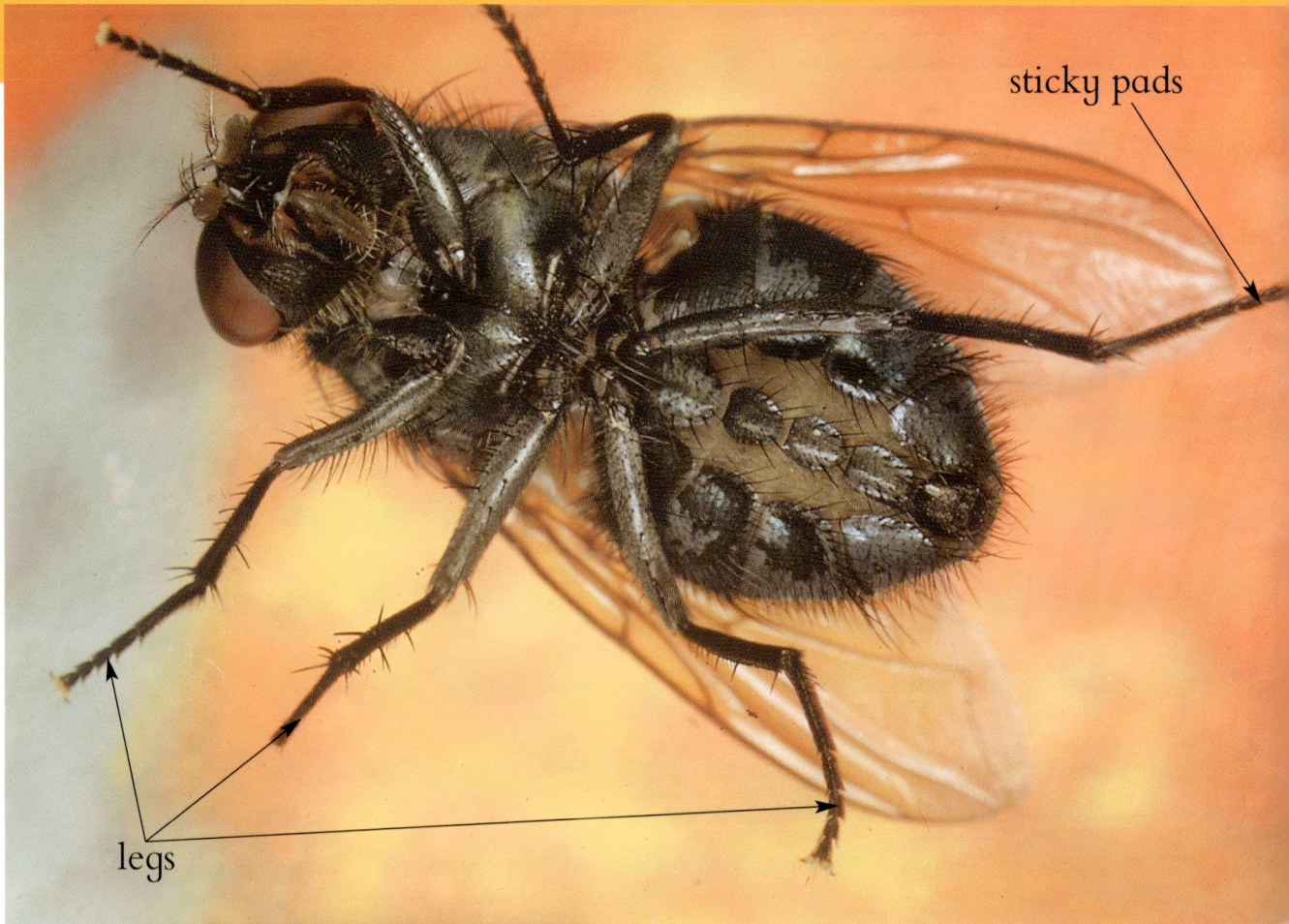

sticky pads

legs

A fly shown from below.

Flies have sticky pads on their feet so that they
can walk up windows. They can also walk
upside down without falling on to the floor.

eyes

A fly's head with its special eyes.

Flies have two very special eyes. The eyes have thousands of small parts. Each of the parts sends a different picture to the flies' brains.

A fly can see all around itself.

Thinking about flies

A fly on some food.

fly

food

See if you can answer these questions about flies.

- What will the fly do to this food so that it will be able to suck it up through its feeding tube?

Housefly eggs.

- If these eggs have just been laid, how long will they take to hatch into **larvae**?

Bug map

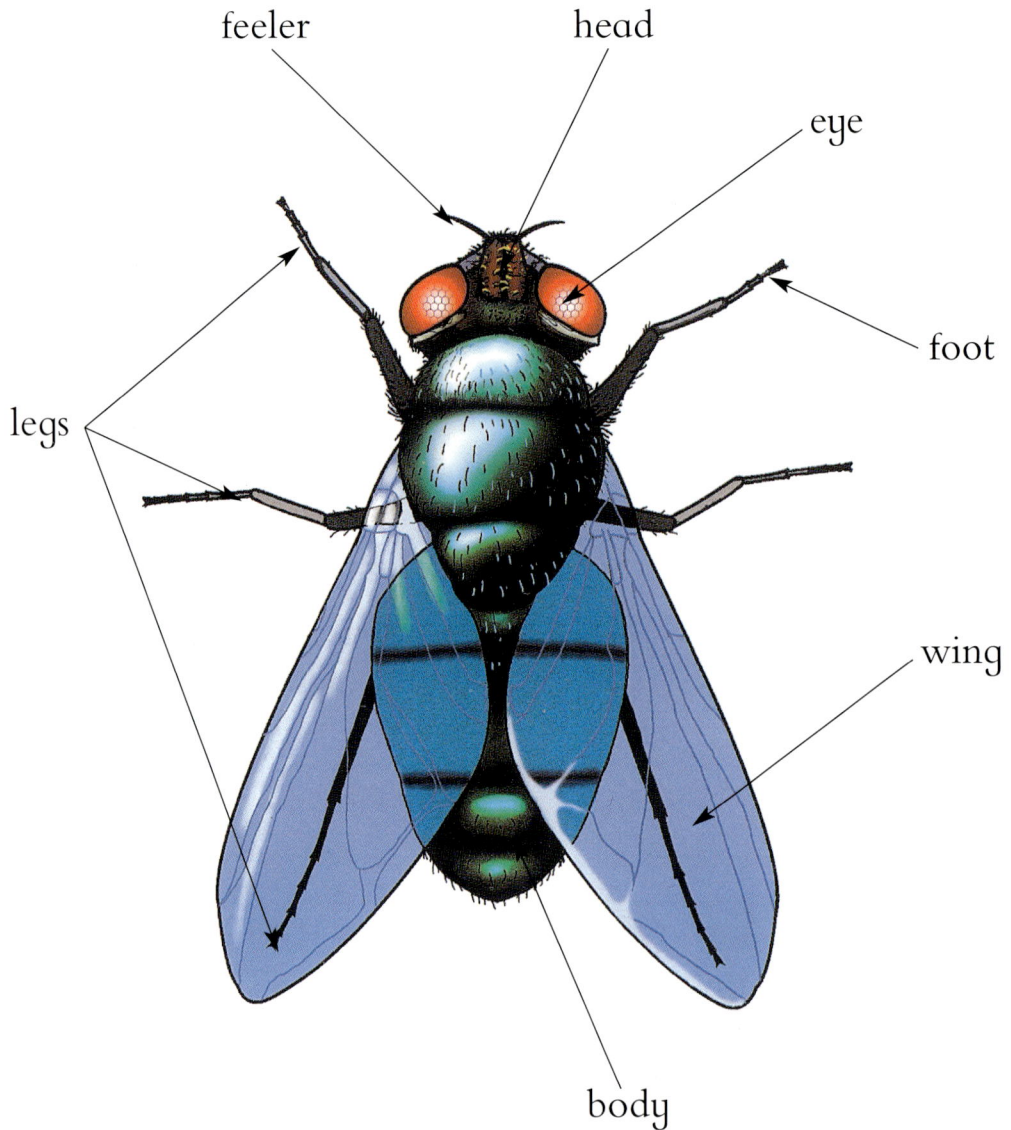

feeler

head

eye

foot

legs

wing

body

Glossary

adult   grown up

droppings the body waste from an animal

decay   rot

feelers   short thin tubes on the fly's head. The fly uses them to smell and feel the air move.

female   girl or mother animal

germ   tiny living thing that can get inside the body and make you ill

insect   a small animal with six legs

larva   the little grub that hatches from an insect egg (more than one = larvae)

male   boy or father animal

mate   when a male and a female come together to make babies

moult   insects do this when they grow too big for their skins. The old skin drops off and a new skin is underneath.

nectar   sweet juice found inside flowers

pest   animal which is a nuisance

pupa   hard case that a larva makes around itself before it turns into an adult fly (more than one = pupae)

swarm   fly very close together in large numbers

a b c d e f g h i j k l m n o p q r s t u v w x y z

Index

Titles in the *Bug Books* series include:

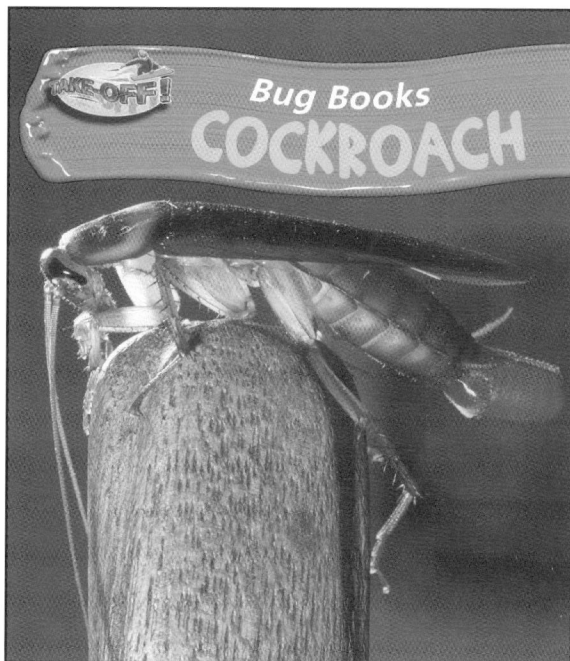

TAKE-OFF!
Bug Books
COCKROACH

Hardback   0 431 01822 7

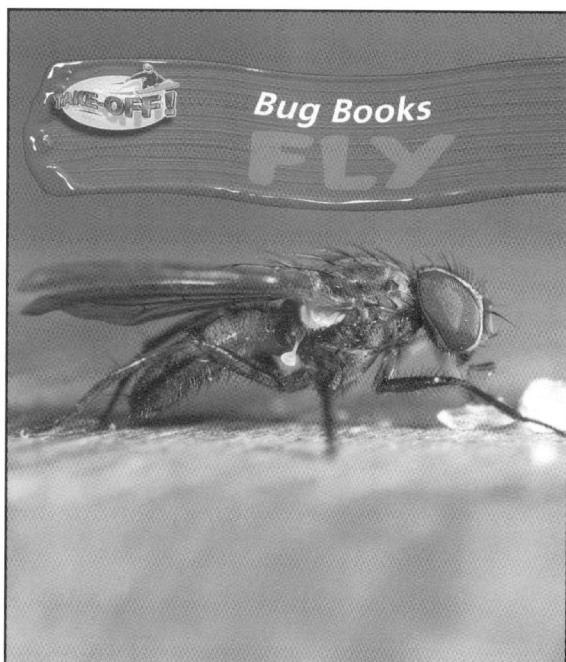

TAKE-OFF!
Bug Books
FLY

Hardback   0 431 01821 9

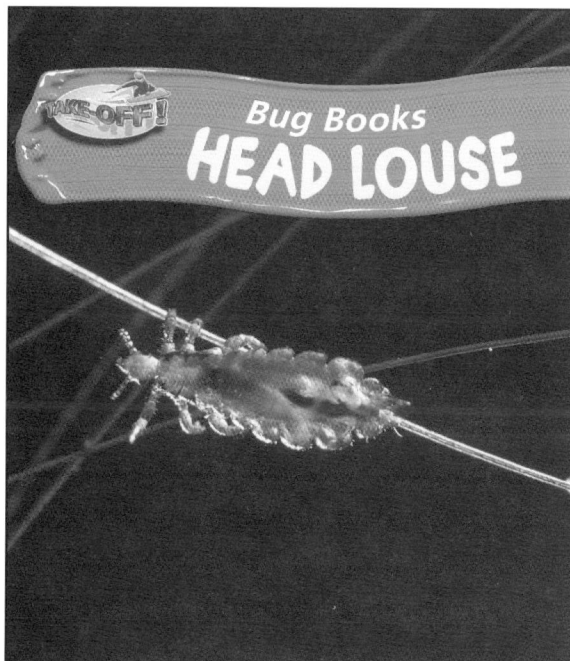

TAKE-OFF!
Bug Books
HEAD LOUSE

Hardback   0 431 01823 5

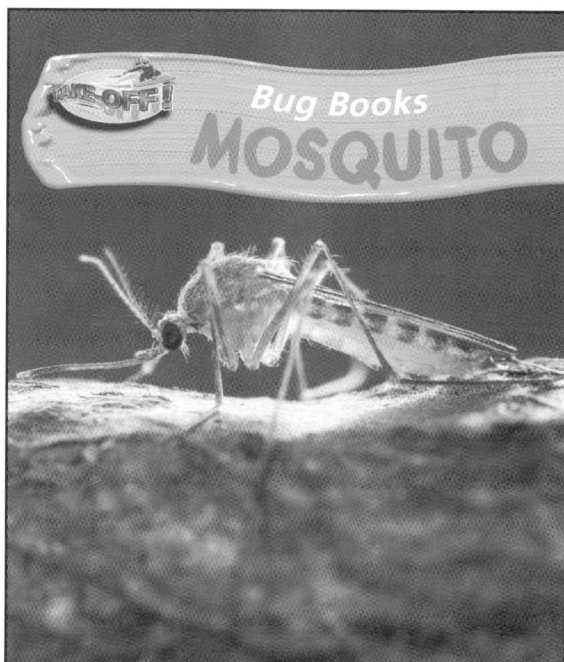

TAKE-OFF!
Bug Books
MOSQUITO

Hardback   0 431 01820 0

Find out about the other titles in this series on our website www.heinemann.co.uk/library